THE CARIBBEAN
TODAY

DOMINICAN REPUBLIC

TURKS
and
CAICOS
(U.K.)

ATLANTIC OCEAN

20°N

• Puerto Plata

North Yaque River

Santiago • • Moca

Escocesa Bay

• San Francisco
de Macorís

HAITI

CORDILLERA CENTRAL

La Vega • *Comú River*

Samaná Bay

• Bonao

**DOMINICAN
REPUBLIC**

San •
Juan

South Yaque River

Enriquillo Lake

Higüey •

Santo Domingo •

San Pedro
de Macorís •

La Romana •

Azua •

Baní •

• San
Cristóbal

Ocoa Bay

Saona Island

Barahona •

18°N

Beata Island

Caribbean Sea

N

W ● E

S

0   20   40 Miles

0   20   40 Kilometers

Mercator Projection

72°W   70°W   68°W

THE CARIBBEAN
TODAY

DOMINICAN REPUBLIC

Bob Temple

Mason Crest Publishers
Philadelphia

Produced by OTTN Publishing, Stockton, N.J.

Mason Crest Publishers
370 Reed Road
Broomall, PA 19008
www.masoncrest.com

First printing

1 3 5 7 9 8 6 4 2

Library of Congress Cataloging-in-Publication Data

Temple, Bob.
  Dominican Republic / Bob Temple.
      p. cm. — (The Caribbean today)
  Includes bibliographical references and index.
  ISBN 978-1-4222-0624-9 (hardcover) — ISBN 978-1-4222-0691-1 (pbk.)
  1. Dominican Republic—Juvenile literature. [1. Dominican Republic.] I. Title.
  F1934.2.T46 2008
  972.93—dc22
                                                    2008032732

THE CARIBBEAN
TODAY

Bahamas
Barbados
Cuba
Dominican Republic
Haiti

Caribbean Islands:
Facts & Figures

Jamaica
Leeward Islands
Puerto Rico
Trinidad & Tobago
Windward Islands

Table of Contents

Discovering the Caribbean

James D. Henderson

THE CARIBBEAN REGION is a lovely, ethnically diverse part of tropical America. It is at once a sea, rivaling the Mediterranean in size; and it is islands, dozens of them, stretching along the sea's northern and eastern edges. Waters of the Caribbean Sea bathe the eastern shores of Central America's seven nations, as well as those of the South American countries Colombia, Venezuela, and Guyana. The Caribbean islands rise, like a string of pearls, from its warm azure waters. Their sandy beaches, swaying palm trees, and balmy weather give them the aspect of tropical paradises, intoxicating places where time seems to stop.

But it is the people of the Caribbean region who make it a unique place. In their ethnic diversity they reflect their homeland's character as a crossroads of the world for more than five centuries. Africa's imprint is most visible in peoples of the Caribbean, but so too is that of Europe. South and East Asian strains enrich the Caribbean ethnic mosaic as well. Some islanders reveal traces of the region's first inhabitants, the Carib and Taino Indians, who flourished there when Columbus appeared among them in 1492.

Though its sparkling waters and inviting beaches beckon tourists from around the globe, the Caribbean islands provide a significant portion of the world's sugar, bananas, coffee, cacao, and natural fibers. They are strategically important also, for they guard the Panama Canal's eastern approaches.

The Caribbean possesses a cultural diversity rivaling the ethnic kaleido-scope that is its human population. Though its dominant culture is Latin American, defined by languages and customs bequeathed it by Spain and France, significant parts of the Caribbean bear the cultural imprint of

The beautiful northeast coast of the Dominican Republic.

Northwestern Europe: Denmark, the Netherlands, and most significantly, Britain.

So welcome to the Caribbean! These lavishly illustrated books survey the human and physical geography of the Caribbean, along with its economic and historical development. Geared to the needs of students and teachers, each of the eleven volumes in the series contains a glossary of terms, a chronology, and ideas for class reports. And each volume contains a recipe section featuring tasty, easy-to-prepare dishes popular in the countries dealt with. Each volume is indexed, and contains a bibliography featuring web sources for further information.

Whether old or young, readers of the eleven-volume series DISCOVERING THE CARIBBEAN will come away with a new appreciation of this tropical sea, its jewel-like islands, and its fascinating and friendly people!

(Opposite) Passengers aboard this cable car, headed up Mount Isabel de Torres, have a spectacular view of the Puerto Plata region. The Dominican Republic has many mountains and fertile valleys. (Right) The sun beams through a cloud forest in the Armando Bermudez National Park.

1 A Tropical Land of Mountains and Valleys

DURING THE FIRST week of December in 1492, Christopher Columbus, who had spent nearly two months exploring Cuba and other islands in what is today called the *West Indies*, sighted an island the Arawak Indians of the region called Bohio. The island's appearance reminded Columbus of his adopted country, Spain. It was, the explorer wrote in his log, "almost like the lands of Castile [a region in Spain], only better." He named the island La Isla Española (the Isle of Spain). Over the years the syllables were run together, and the island acquired the name by which we know it today: *Hispaniola*.

Hispaniola is now home to two different countries—Haiti on the western third, and the Dominican Republic on the eastern two-thirds. The island is located between the Atlantic Ocean and the Caribbean Sea, about 575 miles

9

Quick Facts: The Geography of the Dominican Republic

Location: in the West Indies, covering the eastern two-thirds of the island of Hispaniola, which is between Puerto Rico and Cuba in the Caribbean Sea

Area: (about the size of New Hampshire and Vermont combined)
  total: 18,815 square miles (48,730 sq km)
  land: 18,680 square miles (48,380 sq km)
  water: 135 square miles (350 sq km)

Borders: Haiti, 171 miles (275 km)

Climate: tropical maritime; little seasonal temperature variation; seasonal variation in rainfall

Terrain: rugged highlands and mountains with fertile valleys interspersed

Elevation extremes:
  lowest point: Lago Enriquillo—151 feet (46 meters) below sea level
  highest point: Pico Duarte—10,416 feet (3,175 meters)

Natural hazards: hurricanes, floods

Source: Adapted from CIA World Factbook 2008.

(925 km) southeast of Florida. Cuba, located to the northwest, and Puerto Rico, to the east, are its nearest neighbors. Those three islands and Jamaica make up the *Greater Antilles*, one of three island chains in the West Indies.

The Dominican Republic is the second-largest country in the region, with territory covering 18,815 square miles (48,730 sq km), which makes it about the size of New Hampshire and Vermont combined. Its only border is with Haiti. The Dominican Republic has 800 miles (1,287 km) of coastline.

The land features many mountains and valleys. The Dominican Republic includes both the highest point (Pico Duarte: 10,416 feet, or 3,175 meters) and the lowest point (Lago Enriquillo: 151 feet, or 46 meters, below sea level) in the West Indies.

The Río Yaque del Norte rushes through the Cordillera Central, the country's major mountain range.

Mountains and Valleys

Like many islands, Hispaniola is formed by the peaks of mountains that rise up from the sea floor. In fact, the tallest mountain range in the Dominican Republic, the Cordillera Central, actually stretches from Cuba through Hispaniola and all the way to Puerto Rico—but most of it is underwater.

Mountain ranges divide the Dominican Republic into distinct regions.

The northern portion of the country consists mainly of a coastal plain along the Atlantic Ocean. One smaller mountain range, the Cordillera Septentrional, runs through the area, but its peaks do not exceed 3,500 feet (1,068 meters).

The Cordillera Central, which contains Pico Duarte, is the highest and most majestic mountain range in the West Indies. Its slopes feature thick pine forests.

Between these two mountain ranges lies the Cibao Valley, the most fertile land in the Dominican Republic. The eastern part of the valley is known as the Vega Real, or Royal Meadow. Here coffee, one of the country's main crops, is grown. The Vega Real also supports a wide variety of other crops, including tobacco, rice, corn, and bananas.

Another coastal plain, broken up in the north by the low peaks of the Cordillera Oriental, makes up the eastern portion of the country. Most of the Dominican Republic's sugarcane grows in this region, especially along the southern, or Caribbean, coast. The Caribbean coast is also the site of the nation's capital, Santo Domingo.

Two more mountain ranges, separated by the Neiba Valley, rise up in the southwestern portion of the country. The Sierra de Bahoruco is the southernmost of the two, with the Sierra de Neiba to the north. In between lies mostly desert land, with the exception of the Lake Enriquillo area, which features a swamplike environment.

Several rivers run through the Dominican Republic. The longest is the Yaque del Norte (or North Yaque), which flows from the Cordillera Central near Pico Duarte through the Cibao Valley before emptying into the Atlantic Ocean in the far northwest, near the town of Monte Cristi.

Climate

The Dominican Republic enjoys a *tropical* climate that features warm temperatures and brief periods of rainfall. For the most part, the temperature doesn't vary too much, ranging from a low of about 60°F (16°C) to highs above 90°F (32°C). But some of the lowland areas—particularly those surrounded by mountains—can top 100°F (38°C), as the mountains block

Hurricanes—severe tropical storms with torrential rains and very high winds—are common in the Dominican Republic. In the fall of 1998, Hurricane Georges struck the island. Thousands were left homeless and more than 200 people were killed.

cooling winds. In the upper reaches of the mountains, nighttime temperatures occasionally drop close to freezing (32°F, or 0°C).

An average of about 60 inches (152 cm) of rain falls each year in the Dominican Republic, but this varies by region and can also vary greatly from year to year. Occasional droughts and overly rainy periods have afflicted the country. Generally, the rainy season runs from May to November, but the northern coast also gets rain in December and January.

The Dominican Republic's tropical location puts it in the path of some major storms, including *hurricanes*, primarily during the late summer

A family outside their shack, near San Juan. The Dominican Republic is a poor country; recent figures place one-quarter of the island's population below the poverty line.

months. In 1979, a devastating hurricane killed more than 1,200 citizens of the Dominican Republic and destroyed the homes of another 200,000. In 1998, Hurricane Georges caused more than $1.2 billion in damage to farms, roads, and buildings in the Dominican Republic and killed more than 200 people. Thousands were forced from their homes, which were either damaged by winds or flooded. While Georges was one of the worst, hurricanes hit the Dominican Republic regularly, roughly every two years.

Plants and Animals

The Dominican Republic boasts abundant plant life, including some dense forest and tropical rain forest areas. About half of the country is considered forested, with trees ranging from various types of evergreens to hardwoods such as mahogany and cedar. Palm trees grow near shorelines, and fruit trees, including banana and mango, can also be found. Much of the Dominican Republic's vegetation, however, is not *indigenous*; for example, banana, coffee, and sugarcane were all introduced by the Europeans who first colonized the land, as were various citrus fruit trees.

Some marshy areas are home to crocodiles, and flamingos can occasionally be found in wetlands in and around rain forests. Reptiles, including iguanas, are common. Exotic birds are also seen, but the land of the Dominican Republic is not known for its great variety of animal species. The wetlands and seas are a different story, though. Sea turtles, barracuda, eels, shrimp, red snapper, and mackerel abound. The area is also one of the few remaining homes for the endangered manatee, the gentle "sea cow."

(Opposite) A rainbow shimmers over the excavated remains of the Isabela settlement founded on the island of Hispaniola by Christopher Columbus in 1494. Isabela was abandoned by the Spanish three years later. (Right) Prehistoric rock engravings. The Arawak natives of the island were wiped out by the arrival of the conquistadors.

2 From Pre-Columbian Times to the Present

THE HISTORY OF the Dominican Republic is intertwined with that of Haiti. Today, these neighbors on the island of Hispaniola are very different countries—Haiti has a distinct French influence, while the Dominican Republic's heritage is tied to Spain. But before European colonization of the island—and at various times afterward—the two lands were united culturally or politically.

Pre-Columbian Times and European Discovery

Before Columbus's arrival, the island of Hispaniola was inhabited by a peace-loving group called the Arawak Indians. Historians believe there may have been as many as 500,000 Arawaks living on the island in settlements of

Where Is Columbus Buried?

Where is the final resting place of Christopher Columbus? Both Spain and the Dominican Republic claim that honor, and their disagreement involves a series of events shrouded in the mists of the past.

Each side agrees on certain basic facts. After his death in Valladolid, Spain, in 1506, Columbus's body was buried in a monastery there. Three years later, the admiral's remains were dug up and reburied in another monastery in Seville. When Columbus's oldest son, Diego, died in 1526, Diego's body was buried beside that of his father. Soon, though, Diego's widow petitioned that the remains of father and son be taken to the island of Hispaniola for reburial—as had been Christopher Columbus's wish. In 1537 the royal court of Spain finally granted the request. The remains of Christopher and Diego Columbus were dug up and placed on a ship bound for the Caribbean. Upon arrival on Hispaniola, the two sets of bones were buried in Santo Domingo's cathedral, the father's under the right side of the altar, the son's under the left.

In 1795, however, Spanish authorities ordered Christopher Columbus's remains dug up because they didn't want them to fall into the hands of the French, to whom Spain was ceding its colony of Santo Domingo. The bones were moved to the Spanish colony of Cuba and reburied in the cathedral in Havana. But at the end of the 19th century, in the midst of the

Spain's contender: Seville Cathedral.

Spanish-American War, those remains were dug up yet again, shipped to Spain, and reburied in the cathedral of Seville.

By that time, though, a mystery had emerged in the Dominican Republic. In 1877, workers restoring the cathedral in Santo Domingo discovered a lead coffin buried under the altar. (Whether it was on the right or left side of the altar depended on which way the observer was facing.) The inscription on the coffin referred to the "illustrious and distinguished male,

Dominican claim: Columbus Lighthouse.

Don Cristóbal Colón"—Christopher Columbus's name in Spanish. Might the wrong set of remains—possibly those of Diego Columbus—been dug up in 1795? Dominicans were convinced that's precisely what had happened. But Spaniards insisted that the bones of "the Admiral of the Ocean Seas" rested in the cathedral of Seville.

In October 1992—the 500th anniversary of Columbus's first voyage of discovery, the Dominican Republic moved the remains it claimed were those of the famous explorer from the Cathedral of Santa María la Menor to a new monument. The cross-shaped Faro a Colón (Columbus Lighthouse) stands on the Avenida España in Santo Domingo. The imposing memorial is more than a tourist attraction, however. For the Dominican Republic, being the final resting place of history's most famous explorer is a matter of national pride—though Christopher Columbus's mortal remains may in fact reside in Seville or even, as some historians have suggested, in Cuba.

2,000 or so. They lived primarily as hunter-gatherers and called themselves *Taino,* which means "noble."

But things began to change in 1492. On Christmas Day of that year, Columbus's ship *Santa María* ran aground off the northern coast of what is now Haiti, near the present-day city of Cap-Haïtien. Unable to repair the ship for a return trip to Spain, Columbus ordered his men to strip the vessel of its timbers and use the wood to build a fort on Hispaniola. He called the settlement La Navidad (Spanish for "Christmas").

Columbus left about 40 men at the fort and sailed his remaining two ships back to Spain. There, he gathered supplies and more men to make another *expedition* to the West Indies to claim the gold he believed he would find on Hispaniola.

But when Columbus returned, he discovered that La Navidad had been destroyed and his men killed by the Arawaks. Columbus's second expedition was larger than the first—as many as 1,500 men had made the voyage this time—and the Spaniards soon overcame the native population. Those Indians who didn't die in fighting or from diseases brought by the Europeans found themselves forced to serve the white men on *plantations* and in mines the Spaniards hoped would yield vast amounts of gold.

Among the early settlements established by the Spaniards was La Nueva Isabela, founded in 1496 by Columbus's brother Bartholomew on the site of present-day Santo Domingo. There Christopher Columbus's son Diego built a huge palace called the Alcázar de Colón. Soon thousands of settlers dreaming of riches had flocked to Hispaniola, making the island a center of Spanish rule in the West Indies.

As the native population of Hispaniola died out, the Spaniards imported slaves from Africa to toil in their fields and mines. Soon, the enslaved workforce was almost exclusively African.

The Spaniards' search for gold on Hispaniola—the main reason they originally settled the island—didn't last long. By the mid-1500s, it became clear that other lands in the so-called New World—including Mexico, Peru, and Cuba—offered a much better prospect for obtaining riches. Spanish settlers

An engraving of the late-18th-century slave revolt on Hispaniola, led by Toussaint-Louverture. The success of Toussaint's rebellion would eventually lead to independence for the Dominican Republic (though the country would not be called by that name until 1844).

began bypassing Hispaniola, which became a shadow of its former self, home to only about 30,000 people. Trading ships from Spain largely avoided it, in part because the northern and western portions of the island were infested with pirates. Small merchants in the few operating seaports were of Dutch, French, and English descent.

Santo Domingo, though, had become an important city for Spain. Not only was it a trade hub, it was also considered the central administrative point for Spain's *colonies* in the region. In 1606, Spain ordered all its settlers on Hispaniola to move to the area around Santo Domingo.

In 1697, Spain signed the Treaty of Ryswick with France, giving the French the western third of the island—present-day Haiti. The eastern two-thirds became known as the colony of Santo Domingo. However,

General Rafael Trujillo (center), pictured here with his family reviewing troops during a military parade, wielded great power in the Dominican Republic from 1930 to 1961.

Spain's concentration on its other colonies in the New World helped bring about Santo Domingo's decline. Eventually, Spain lost interest in Santo Domingo entirely. It ceded the colony to the French in 1795.

Revolutions

Only four years earlier, black slaves in Haiti, led by Toussaint-Louverture, had risen up against their French colonial masters. By 1801, they gained control of the entire island of Hispaniola. Toussaint set all the slaves free and established a constitution. For several years, France battled for control of the island, but ultimately withdrew all of its troops in 1803. Jean-Jacques Dessalines declared the independence of Haiti in 1804, becoming the country's emperor.

In 1809 Spain regained control of the eastern part of Hispaniola, but its rule there proved ineffective. Consequently Spain granted Santo Domingo its independence in 1821. Santo Domingo's independence did not last long, as Haiti invaded and took control of the country in 1822. The Haitians maintained control of the entire island until 1844, a period that saw the Spanish-speaking side of Hispaniola fall further into decline.

Juan Pablo Duarte led a revolt against Haiti in 1844 that reclaimed the Spanish-speaking two-thirds of the island. The newly formed Dominican Republic declared its independence on February 27, 1844.

Independence

As is the case with many young nations, the Dominican Republic's independence didn't bring an end to political strife. For 17 years, two generals, Pedro Santana and Buenaventura Báez Méndez, fought for control of the country. The internal strife, and the continued fear of another Haitian invasion, prompted the country to ask Spain to govern it, which Spain did from 1861 to 1865.

Years of political chaos followed Spain's departure. Eventually, Ulises Heureaux took power and ruled the country as a *dictator* from 1882 to 1889. He left the country with huge unpaid debts to foreign nations. From 1905 until 1941, the United States took over the collection of customs duties in the Dominican Republic and oversaw the repayment of the debts. Beginning in 1916, the U.S. Marines kept order in the country.

A military revolt allowed Rafael Leónidas Trujillo Molina to take control of the Dominican Republic in 1930. He ruled for 30 years as a dictator, limiting freedoms and prosecuting or killing his political opponents. The country improved economically, but most of the money generated was funneled to the Trujillo family's interests. This didn't benefit the country's struggling citizens.

When Trujillo was assassinated in 1961, another power struggle erupted. Juan Bosch was elected president in December 1962, but the military and the country's upper-class leaders overthrew him a year later. The military formed a three-member council, called a *junta*, to govern the Dominican Republic.

When rebels who supported Bosch attempted to take control again in 1965, the United States intervened to restore order, preventing Bosch's return. A truce was declared in May 1965. In June 1966, Joaquín Balaguer was elected president, and in September of that year, the last U.S. troops left the Dominican Republic.

The Dominican Republic's president, Leonel Fernández, gives a speech after receiving the presidential sash at the national congress in Santo Domingo, August 16, 2008.

Early in Balaguer's first 12 years in office, high sugar prices brought money into the Dominican economy. But when sugar prices declined, the economy deteriorated. Balaguer lost much of his support. He was defeated by Silvestre Antonio Guzmán Fernández in 1978, but regained the presidency in 1986 and served until 1996. In that year's election, Balaguer supported Leonel Fernández, who won the presidency with 51 percent of the vote.

In 2000, Rafael Hipólito Mejía Domínguez was elected to a four-year presidential term. However, during his administration the country suffered through an economic crisis. This led to Mejía's defeat in the 2004 election by Leonel Fernández.

After taking office in 2004, Fernández focused on restructuring the country's economy to make it more stable. His administration also worked to develop new industries in the Dominican Republic. In 2008, Fernández was elected to a third presidential term with 54 percent of the vote.

Though the country's economy has diversified in recent years, agriculture remains an important way of life for many Dominicans. (Opposite) Farms in the Cordillera Central of the Dominican Republic. (Right) The towers and buildings of the La Romana sugar mill, located next to the Río Dulce.

3 The Economy: Not Just Sugar Anymore

OVERALL, THE LAST 20 years have seen a marked improvement in economic conditions in the Dominican Republic. In 2007, according to estimates from the World Bank, a development organization, the Dominican Republic's *gross domestic product (GDP)* reached $56.4 billion. This meant that the Dominican Republic has a larger economy than any other Caribbean country, and one of the largest economies in Latin America. (GDP is the total value of goods and services produced in a country annually.) Per capita GDP in the Dominican Republic—each Dominican's average share of the country's annual economic activity—was estimated at $5,334 in 2007. While this does not sound like much by U.S. standards, when compared to all nations the Dominican Republic ranks as a lower-middle-income country.

Still, income inequality remains a problem. Wealth is concentrated in the hands of relatively few people. The richest 10 percent take home 40 percent of the country's income; meanwhile, just one-fifth of the country's income goes to the poorest 50 percent of the population. The country also shoulders a difficult burden: its debts to other nations total more than $8.4 billion.

The Dominican Republic is still recovering from a banking crisis in 2003, in which three of the country's major banks failed. The government borrowed money to bail out the banks. However, this led to price inflation. The value of the country's currency, the Dominican peso, dropped sharply, making goods and services more expensive. The high rate of inflation—estimated as high as 27 percent in 2004—had a great impact on the living standards of the country's residents, in particular those living at or near the poverty line.

Since taking office in 2004, the administration of President Leonel Fernández has attempted to stabilize the country's economy. By 2008, the inflation rate had dropped to about 6 percent. This helped the Dominican Republic's economy begin to grow again in 2007 and 2008.

Another boost to the economy occurred after March 2007, when the Dominican Republic implemented a trade agreement with the United States and five Central American countries. The Dominican Republic-Central America Free Trade Agreement (DR-CAFTA) reduces or eliminates tariffs on imports and exports, making foreign trade more profitable for all parties involved.

Agricultural Roots

Historically, the Dominican Republic has been primarily an exporter of agricultural products—specifically sugarcane. Although in recent years the country has tried to transition its economy to focus more on industry and technology, the Dominican Republic remains largely agricultural. Including those who own small farms, roughly half of all Dominicans are involved in farming. Most of those are *subsistence farmers*, people who live off the crops they grow for themselves. Some also operate as *sharecroppers*. Large plantations employ about 17 percent of the country's workforce.

Sugarcane remains the Dominican Republic's main crop for *export*. About 75 percent of the nearly one million metric tons of sugar grown in the country each year gets exported to the United States; most of the remainder stays within the Dominican Republic.

The Dominican Republic also grows and exports tobacco, coffee, and cotton. Other significant crops include rice, beans, bananas, avocados, mangoes, and oranges. Dominican planters also cultivate cacao beans, which are used to make cocoa and chocolate. The Dominican Republic has become one of the top ten cocoa exporters in the world.

In 2003 and 2004, the value of the Dominican peso dropped sharply. The government has taken action to stabilize the country's currency.

In addition, the country produces livestock, including some beef cattle that are exported to the United States. Dominicans also raise dairy cattle and export some dairy products; eggs are exported as well.

Tourism in the Dominican Republic

Today, tourism brings more money into the Dominican Republic than any other industry, including sugar exporting. Almost 4 million people visit

A group of Dominican children watch from the beach at Barahona as fishermen bring in their catch in the early morning.

A surfer rides the waves off one of the Dominican Republic's north-eastern beaches. Today tourism-related jobs employ many Dominicans.

the country each year, making it one of the most popular destinations in the Caribbean.

The major resort areas are at Puerto Plata, in the northern part of the country; along the eastern coast at Punta Cana and Bavaro; and in the south at Bayahibe.

Industry

Industry has also seen strong gains in recent years. Much of this can be attributed to the *free-trade zones* the Dominican Republic has established within its borders. These areas allow foreign businesses to operate in the country inexpensively by reducing or eliminating the duties and taxes they might ordinarily pay for imports and exports. Nearly 500 businesses have taken advantage of these zones, allowing the country to reduce its unemployment rate and improve economic conditions. Goods produced (gar-

Quick Facts: The Economy of the Dominican Republic

Gross domestic product (GDP*):
$56.4 billion
GDP per capita: $5,334
Inflation: 6.1%
Natural resources: gold, nickel, clay, gypsum, limestone, salt
Agriculture (11.7% of GDP): sugarcane, coffee, cotton, cocoa, tobacco, rice, beans, potatoes, corn, bananas; cattle, pigs, dairy products, beef, eggs
Services (64.4% of GDP): banking, government, other
Industry (23.8% of GDP): tourism, sugar processing, ferronickel and gold mining, textiles, cement, tobacco
Foreign trade:
Exports—$7.24 billion: ferronickel, sugar, gold, silver, coffee, cocoa, tobacco, meats, consumer goods.
Imports—$13.82 billion: foodstuffs, cotton and other fabrics, petroleum, chemicals, pharmaceuticals.
Currency exchange rate:
34.96 Dominican pesos = U.S. $1 (2008)

* GDP or gross domestic product = the total value of goods and services produced in a year.

Figures are 2007 estimates unless otherwise noted.
Sources: World Bank; CIA World Factbook 2008.

ments, medical devices) or processed (sugar, coffee, cacao, and tobacco) in the free-trade zones make up about 70 percent of the value of the country's exports.

About half of the companies that participate are *textile* or garment manufacturers. The Dominican Republic has more than 250 apparel plants. They produce such items as jeans and other denim products, men's and women's undergarments, polo shirts, shorts, dress shirts, blazers, fur coats, and leather jackets.

Other companies set up in duty-free zones manufacture shoes, cigars, jewelry, components for electronic equipment, and hospital supplies. The government's aggressive promotion of duty-free zones has spurred the growth of the industrial sector of the Dominican economy. In all, about one-fourth of the labor force is employed in industrial jobs, including sugar processing.

Mining

Gold and silver were on Columbus's mind when he arrived on Hispaniola in the late 15th century. Those minerals are still mined today, albeit on a relatively small scale. The mineral ferronickel (iron-nickel) is the biggest target of mining operations in the country now. Dominican mining operations also extract other substances, including bauxite (used to make aluminum), clay, gypsum, limestone, and salt. Today, however, mining is a very minor sector of the economy, employing less than 1 percent of the labor force.

(Opposite) Men play bamboo drums during a street festival. Music is an important part of life in the Dominican Republic. (Right) A local priest leads worshippers in a Christmas celebration near the church at San Gabriel. Some 95 percent of the population is Roman Catholic.

4 A Blend of Spanish and African

THE DOMINICAN REPUBLIC is a blend of two cultures, neither of them indigenous to the country, as the Arawak Indians who originally inhabited the island of Hispaniola were virtually eliminated by the Spanish colonists. Today, the Spanish influence can be seen in nearly every aspect of Dominican society, mixed with a strong dose of African traditions brought by black slaves.

Mulattoes, or people of mixed European and African heritage, make up almost three-fourths of the Dominican Republic's citizens. Only 16 percent of Dominicans are white, and 11 percent are black.

Status in the Dominican Republic is often determined by the color of one's skin. Those who have darker skin are frequently referred to as Haitians, even though they may not be of Haitian origin. (The term carries negative connotations in the Dominican Republic, where bitterness lingers over Haiti's 19th-century invasions.) In the 1980s, many Haitians did immigrate to the Dominican Republic in search of agricultural work. And because of Haiti's recent history of political instability and its chronic poverty, immigration to the Dominican Republic continues.

Dominican society is sharply divided along class lines. An upper class of landowners and business owners controls a disproportionate amount of the country's wealth: 10 percent of the population receives 40 percent of the total income generated. Below the upper class is the middle class, consisting of urban shopkeepers, professionals, and government workers, among others. The large lower class consists of rural farmers and urban poor who are either unemployed or working for very low wages in an industrial setting.

Education

A system of *compulsory* education established in the 1950s has improved the *literacy* rate in the Dominican Republic. The system, which is overseen by a government agency, requires children to go to primary school starting at age seven and continuing for at least six years. Unfortunately, educational problems persist. The education system lacks money to pay teachers, buy books and other supplies, and build schools. In rural areas, these problems are magnified. Still, about 87 percent of Dominicans aged 15 or older are able to read and write.

Secondary schools are available, but not required, for Dominican children. There are two types of secondary schools: those designed to prepare students for college, and those that teach a specific trade or vocation. Most

Quick Facts: The People of the Dominican Republic

Population: 9,507,133

Ethnic groups: mulatto (mixed black and white descent), 73%; white, 16%; black, 11%

Age structure:
0–14 years: 31.8%
15–64 years: 62.4%
65 years and over: 5.8%

Population growth rate: 1.495%

Birth rate: 22.65 births/1,000 population

Death rate: 5.3 deaths/1,000 population

Infant mortality rate: 26.93 deaths/1,000 live births

Life expectancy at birth:

total population: 73.39 years
male: 71.61 years
female: 75.24 years

Total fertility rate: 2.78 children born per woman

Religions: Roman Catholic, 95%; other religions include Protestant, Jewish, and voodoo

Languages: Spanish (official)

Literacy rate (age 15 and older): 87% (2002 census)

All figures are 2008 estimates unless otherwise indicated.
Source: Adapted from CIA World Factbook 2008.

students enrolled in secondary schools attend the six-year program designed to prepare them for college. Upper-class Dominicans typically send their children to private secondary schools. Yet fewer than half of all children in the country attend secondary school, in part because children are legally able to work on farms and in other jobs when they reach 14 years of age.

Health

Although large cities and towns enjoy the services of hospitals and doctors, many residents of rural areas have almost no access to health care. In addition, inadequate sanitary and nutrition practices in poor rural and urban areas make disease outbreaks common. Because of these problems, the Dominican Republic's infant mortality rate remains fairly high. Nearly five times more babies die before reaching their first birthday in the Dominican Republic than in the United States. Still, overall health conditions in the country continue to improve, and life expectancies are climbing. Although about 2 percent of Dominicans are infected with *HIV*, the virus that causes

Men dressed in colorful traditional costume take part in a festival in Cabral. The festival, which takes place on the Christian holiday Good Friday, includes dancing and parades.

AIDS, the country's AIDS problem is not nearly as severe as that of neighboring Haiti.

Language

The national language of the Dominican Republic is Spanish, which was, of course, brought to the country by the colonists who took control of Hispaniola beginning in the late 15th century. As descendants of the first Spanish colonists in the New World, the people of the Dominican Republic are proud of their Spanish heritage. They speak a form of the language that is very close to that spoken in Spain.

Religion

The Spanish colonists brought more than their language with them to the New World; they also brought their religion, Roman Catholicism. The Catholic Church gained its first New World foothold in the West Indies, and specifically on Hispaniola. In fact, the Dominican Republic was the site of the first Catholic Mass celebrated in the New World, in 1493.

Priests of the Dominican Order were important in the early social life of Hispaniola, and of Spanish America generally. In the year 1511 Friar Antonio de Montesinos preached a fiery Christmas Day sermon in the cathedral of Santo Domingo. In it he angered the Spanish settlers by denouncing their cruelty toward their Indian workers. Sixteen years later one of his listeners, Bartolomé de Las Casas, joined the Dominican Order. Las Casas went on to become a famous crusader for Indian rights throughout Spanish America. The Spanish queen Isabella named Las Casas her "Protector of the Indians."

Today Catholicism is so entrenched in Dominican life that the Bible is at the center of the country's coat of arms. Roughly 95 percent of the people are Roman Catholic, and the Dominican government actively promotes the Church. Other religions are tolerated, and the Dominican Republic has small Protestant and Jewish communities, along with some practitioners of voodoo. The latter group is composed primarily of immigrants from Haiti, where voodoo's influence is profound.

Arts and Culture

Music and dance are at the center of Dominican arts and culture. The music features the hard thump of the African drumbeat, mixed with the maracas, guitars, and other stringed instruments of Spain. The national dance, the merengue, is primarily of African origin. Its rhythmic movements are accentuated by the colorful floral-patterned dresses worn by the women.

The country is also known for handcrafted woodcarvings, which are sold in markets around Santo Domingo. Also sold are pottery and ceramic items made by Dominican artisans, mainly women. Santo Domingo is the country's cultural center, offering museums dedicated to history and art, as well as the National School of Fine Arts.

Literature has long been important to the Dominican people, and a number of noted writers and poets have called the country home. Salomé Ureña de Henríquez (1850–1897) was an acclaimed poet whose sons, Pedro Henríquez Ureña (1884–1946) and Max Henríquez Ureña (1883–1968), were important writers, critics, and educators. Manuel de Jesús Galván (1834–1910) wrote the book often considered the most famous in the

Paintings in an open-air gallery in the Dominican Republic.

country's history. The novel, *Enriquillo*, is the story of an Indian uprising against Spanish colonists.

Recreation and Entertainment

Soccer (or in Spanish, *fútbol*) is the main sport in much of Latin America (and, in fact, in much of the world), but the Dominican Republic has an extraordinary passion for baseball. Amazingly, the small country produces more professional baseball players than any country in the world

One baseball star who grew up in the Dominican Republic is pitcher Pedro Martinez. The right-handed pitcher has won more than 200 games and received the Cy Young Award, given each year to the best pitcher in the American and National Leagues, three times: in 1997, 1999, and 2000.

except the United States. At the beginning of the 2002 season, about 200 Dominican players were on major-league rosters. Many of them return to the Dominican Republic in the winter to play in Dominican professional leagues.

Many of the players grew up in and around Santo Domingo. But one small town, San Pedro de Macorís, has produced an unusually high number of professional players for a city its size. Baseball stars from San Pedro de Macorís include Alfonso Soriano, Robinson Cano, and Sammy Sosa.

Other major-league stars from the Dominican Republic include pitcher Pedro Martinez, outfielders Vladimir Guerrero and Manny Ramirez, and infielders Albert Pujols, Miguel Tejada, Adrian Beltre, and Rafael Furcal.

Children also play soccer, volleyball, and basketball, while adults engage in another activity, cockfighting. In this spectator sport, roosters that are bred to be aggressive battle each other, usually to the death. Spectators bet on which rooster will win.

(Opposite) An aerial view of Santo Domingo and the Ozama River. Santo Domingo, the capital of the Dominican Republic, is the largest city in the country. (Right) Squalid conditions in the country's interior.

5 Important Cities and Communities

THE DOMINICAN REPUBLIC has only one large city—Santo Domingo, the capital. Much of the rest of the country is rural, although many small cities have unique features and fascinating histories.

Santo Domingo

This capital city is the heart of the Dominican Republic. It is the most important commercial and industrial center, due in part to nearby hydroelectric dams, which provide businesses with inexpensive electricity. The city's port is the country's busiest, as is its international airport. The cultural life of the Dominican Republic revolves around Santo Domingo as well. The city boasts several universities and schools for the arts, museums, and a symphony orchestra. With a population of about 2.3 million, Santo

Domingo provides a home for nearly 25 percent of the Dominican Republic's people.

Santo Domingo lies near the center of the Dominican Republic's southern coast, where the Ozama and Isabella Rivers empty into the Caribbean Sea. The oldest continuously occupied city in the Western Hemisphere, it was founded in 1496 by Bartholomew Columbus, the brother of Christopher Columbus. There a son of Christopher Columbus, Diego, also constructed the first palace built by European colonists in the New World. The palace, called the Alcázar de Colón, is located high on a slope that overlooks the port. The restored early-16th-century structure is now a popular tourist attraction.

Another popular area for tourists is the Colonial Zone, the site of Bartholomew Columbus's original settlement. It has been restored and includes foundations of the original buildings, which were constructed as many as five centuries ago.

Like most major cities, Santo Domingo also has poor areas. In these sections of the city, small shacks constructed of corrugated metal and other flimsy materials provide shelter for residents crowded together in squalid conditions. Santo Domingo's population more than doubled in the last two decades of the 20th century, and the rapid growth strained—and in some cases overwhelmed—the city's ability to provide basic services, such as water, sewer, and police protection, in certain neighborhoods.

Happily, life in Santo Domingo has been improving. Government efforts to promote tourism have led to improvements in the city's *infrastructure*. And tourism, in turn, has pumped money into the local economy. Now, along with its historic structures from centuries past, Santo Domingo features high-rise apartment buildings, modern hotels, and palm-lined boulevards with shops, restaurants, and clubs. Santo Domingo has also preserved large open spaces, including some beautiful parks, within its city limits.

Santiago

Santiago de los Caballeros, the Dominican Republic's second-largest city, is located in the north-central part of the country. It is the capital of the Santiago province. Other than Santo Domingo, Santiago de los Caballeros is the only city

The Obelisk of Santo Domingo is located at the city's primary waterfront business area, El Malecón, which attracts many visitors to its hotels, restaurants, and shops. In 1997 the mural was painted on the obelisk; it depicts three sisters killed in 1960 by the secret police of former dictator Rafael Trujillo.

in the country that could be considered metropolitan. Still, it doesn't offer many of the conveniences residents of the world's major cities have come to expect.

By 2008, its population was nearly a million people, but in many respects Santiago de los Caballeros continues to resemble a town more than a city. The pace of life is much less hectic than in Santo Domingo, and Santiago's residents retain a distinctly laid-back demeanor.

A row of houses on a dusty road in the village of Honda Valle. Millions of Dominicans live in rural villages like this one. Many of the people living in rural villages are poor and do not have access to clean water.

Santiago de los Caballeros has long been home to some of the richest people in the Dominican Republic. Located in the heart of the lush Cibao Valley, it is also the site of cigar manufacturing plants fed by the tobacco grown in the area.

Puerto Plata

This small city has become a tourist center, due in part to its location on the scenic northern coast near Mount Isabel de Torres. Puerto Plata, which means "Silver Port," was originally settled in 1494 by Christopher Columbus, who called the settlement Isabela.

In the last 30 years, government improvements have made the area much more visitor-friendly. Now the seaside city attracts vacationers with its picturesque walkways, parks, hotels, and resorts. Besides tourism, the town's economy thrives on sugarcane: an abundance of fields in the surrounding area are dedicated to the cultivation of the crop.

Like Puerto Plata, a number of other small, coastal towns have grown because of the influence of tourism. However, the heart of the Dominican Republic has remained largely rural and agricultural in nature.

A Calendar of Dominican Festivals

Most of the Dominican Republic's biggest festivals and parades revolve around religious holidays. Because the country's population is overwhelmingly Catholic, the most important festivals celebrate saints' days and other religious events.

January

On January 1, Dominicans, like people all over the world, celebrate **New Year's Day.**

Epiphany, also known as **Three Kings' Day**, is a Catholic celebration on January 6 that marks the visit of the three kings, or Magi, to the baby Jesus. In the Dominican Republic, children receive gifts from the Magi rather than from Santa Claus.

On the 21st, Dominican Catholics honor **Nuestra Señora de Altagracia** (Our Lady of Altagracia). Veneration of the Virgin Mary under this name dates to 1502 and involves a late-15th- or early-16th-century portrait of Mary and Jesus that was probably brought to Hispaniola from Spain.

On January 26, Dominicans celebrate **Juan Pablo Duarte's Birthday**. Known as "the Father of the Dominican Republic," Duarte planned a revolution that led to the country's independence.

February

Carnival, a festival that started in medieval Europe as the final celebration before the Christian season of Lent, is observed on February 26 and 27 in the Dominican Republic. During Carnival, Dominicans dress up in colorful costumes and wear imaginative masks. In Santiago, the masks are decorated with shells or jewels. In Monte Cristi, the masks look like bulls. In Santo Domingo, the heart of the Carnival celebration, dancers' masks may have horns and a duck's bill, or may represent various traditional characters or superstitions.

February 27, when Carnival activities in the Dominican Republic climax, is doubly festive because it is also **Independence Day**. In the late afternoon, a parade filled with floats and characters in crazy costumes snakes through the streets of Santo Domingo. Leading the festivities are a king and queen of the celebration. Independence Day also involves lots of dancing and food.

March

The Christian holy days of **Good Friday** and **Easter** may fall in March or April, depending on the particular year's lunar cycle. Many communities in the Dominican Republic host special events on these days. In Santo Domingo, Catholics take wooden images of Jesus Christ from the church and march through the streets with the Christ figure at the front of the crowd.

April

April 14: **Pan-American Day**

May

May 1: **Labor Day**

A Calendar of Dominican Festivals

July

Santo Domingo hosts the **Merengue Festival** each year in late July. Celebrating the popular dance, the festival—held outdoors on the city's waterfront—attracts the best Dominican and Latin American musicians. So many dancers crowd the streets that cars have difficulty passing!

August

August 5 is **Foundation Day**, when residents of Santo Domingo celebrate the founding of their city.

August 16, **Restoration Day,** celebrates the Dominican Republic's breaking away from Haitian control.

September

On September 24, Catholics in the Dominican Republic observe **Our Lady of Mercy Day**, which celebrates the life of Mary, the mother of Jesus Christ.

October

October 12: **Columbus Day**
October 24: **United Nations Day**

November

On November 1, Dominican Catholics celebrate **All Saints' Day**, in honor of the Church's saints.

November 6 is **Constitution Day** in the Dominican Republic.

December

In the Dominican Republic, as in other predominantly Christian countries, **Christmas** is a major holiday. Americans would find much about the Dominican Christmas season familiar, including gift giving; Nativity scenes in churches; celebrations with family, coworkers, and friends; and sometimes even Christmas trees! Many Dominican Catholics attend midnight Mass on Christmas Eve. The following week is filled with special dinners and dances. The celebration ends on Three Kings' Day, January 6.

Recipes

Mangu

(Serves 6)
3 large, green plantains
1 1/2 oz. salt
1/2 quart boiling water
2 oz. olive oil
6 oz. sliced white onion
6 oz. sliced Cuban or Anaheim peppers

Directions:
1. Wash the plantains and boil them for about 20 minutes. Cooking time will depend on the age of each plantain and its size. You will be preparing a puree, so make sure the plantains are fully but not overly cooked.
2. Let the plantains cool a bit. Remove the skins and place the plantains in a bowl. Salt them, add the boiling water, then mash them.
3. Transfer the mashed plantains to a food processor or heavy-duty blender and finish the pureeing.
4. Sauté the onions and peppers in the olive oil.
5. Put the puree in a serving dish, top it with the sautéed onion and pepper mixture, and serve.

Black Bean Soup

(Serves 10 people)
2 pounds washed black beans
1 oz. diced garlic
1 lb diced white onions
4 oz. chopped celery
1/2 lb Cuban or Anaheim peppers
1 lb white rice
1/2 bunch of fresh cilantro

Directions:
1. Wash beans well and soak them in water overnight.
2. Lightly sauté garlic, onions, celery, and peppers. This is referred to as a *sofrito*.
3. Bring beans to a boil, add *sofrito*, rice, and fresh cilantro, and simmer for four hours.

Corn Pudding

(Serves 10 people)
2 cans (15 oz. each) of creamed corn
2 quarts milk
1/2 lb granulated sugar
1 vanilla bean
2 oz. ground cinnamon
2 oz. cornstarch

Directions:
1. Using a blender, combine the creamed corn and half the milk.
2. Pass the corn and milk through a medium mesh strainer, then put it in a pan. Add the rest of the milk, the sugar, and the vanilla bean and bring the mixture to a boil.
3. Reduce to a simmer, add the cinnamon, and cook gently for 10 minutes.
4. Dissolve cornstarch in a bit of water and add.
5. When pudding has thickened, turn off heat at once, remove vanilla bean, and pour the pudding into individual cups or serving bowls. Dust with ground cinnamon. Do not refrigerate before serving.

Dominican Vanilla Cake

(For two cakes)
1 lb butter
10 whole eggs
1 lb granulated sugar
1 1/2 lbs cake flour
Dash of salt
1/2 oz. baking powder
1/2 oz. vanilla extract
1 cup fresh orange juice

Directions:
1. Cream butter and sugar together for about 10 minutes at a medium-high speed using an electric mixer.
2. Add eggs, five at a time, to the mixture. After each addition, beat for about one minute.
3. Sift cake flour, salt, and baking powder together and then add them to the previous ingredients. Mix and combine batter for five minutes at medium speed.
4. Add the vanilla extract and the orange juice and continue to mix for about two more minutes.
5. Bake cake in a preheated oven at 400 degrees until a toothpick inserted into cake comes out dry.

from CyberChefs Electronic Union:
www.marscafe.com/Php/downloads/files/php

[Original Content c. 2001, Premier-Net.com, Last revised: March 18, 2001]

Glossary

colony—an area of land ruled by a distant country.

compulsory—required; mandatory.

dictator—a leader who holds sole power in a country and frequently rules in a brutal fashion.

expedition—a journey for a particular purpose, such as to discover or explore uncharted land.

export—a product that is manufactured or produced in one country but sold to a foreign country.

free-trade zone—in the Dominican Republic, an area in which businesses can operate without paying most of the duties and taxes imposed on exports and imports.

Greater Antilles—the island chain that includes Cuba, Hispaniola, Jamaica, and Puerto Rico.

gross domestic product (GDP)—the total value of goods and services produced within a country in a one-year period.

Hispaniola—the island occupied by Haiti and the Dominican Republic.

HIV—the virus that causes AIDS, a disease characterized by a weakened immune system.

hurricane—a strong storm featuring winds as high as 150 miles (241 km) per hour, heavy rainfall, and, frequently, dangerous lightning.

indigenous—native or original to a certain area.

infrastructure—the system of public works (including roads, bridges, water and sewer services, and the electrical-power grid) of a city, region, or country.

Glossary

junta—a council that controls a government after power has been taken by military force.

literacy—the ability to read and write.

plantation—a large tract of land devoted to agriculture, especially one that was worked by slaves.

sharecropper—a farmer who works on land owned by another in exchange for a portion of the crops.

subsistence farming—the cultivation of a usually quite small area of land for the purpose of feeding one's own family.

tropical—the frost-free portion of the globe with temperatures high enough to permit year-round plant growth.

textile—a woven or knit cloth.

West Indies—an area in the Caribbean made up of three different island chains: the Greater Antilles, the Lesser Antilles, and the Bahamas.

Project and Report Ideas

Flashcards

Create flashcards from the glossary terms in this book. Put the term on one side of the card and the definition on the other. Choose a person to say the term out loud while the rest of the group takes turns giving the definitions. Break into two teams and challenge each other by trying to get the most consecutive correct answers.

Flag poster

Make your own flag representing the Dominican Republic. Pick a piece of colored construction paper as your background. Then try to think of at least three things that represent the Dominican Republic, and paste them into the middle of your flag. You can create those out of construction paper, cut them out of a magazine, or print them off the Internet. Next, find a picture of the real flag of the Dominican Republic. Create a copy of that flag using construction paper and other materials. Paste both finished flags onto a large piece of white poster board so you can compare them. Leave space for a page beneath the flags. Then write a page explaining why you chose the shapes for your flag and what the differences are between your flag and the real one. Try to find out the history behind the flag of the Dominican Republic and include that in your report. Paste your finished report on the poster board underneath the two flags. Hang the finished poster on a wall in your classroom for everyone to see.

Create a clay model of the Dominican Republic

Clay is one of the Dominican Republic's most common natural resources. Create a model of the country in clay. Look at a topographical map (a map that shows the height of the land), and a map that shows the type of surface land (forest, farmland, urban) to see how you should make your model. Use different colors of clay to indicate different types of areas, such as brown for the mountains, green for the forests, and blue for lakes and rivers. Make sure the highest mountain, Pico Duarte, is the highest point on your model, and Lake Enriquillo is the lowest point.

Create a Dominican Republic resource page on the Web

Surf the Internet and find websites related to the Dominican Republic. Choose the most interesting ones and compile a list. Your class can put the links on its own Web page for others to use. Make sure to write a few sentences about each website so people know what type of information it contains.

Find out more

Write a one-page report on any of the following:

- An animal that calls the Dominican Republic home. Talk about what it looks like, where it can be found, what it eats, and other details you find interesting.
- Polished amber jewelry is popular with tourists who visit the Dominican Republic. Research where amber comes from and what it looks like. What other parts of the world produce amber?
- Who was Juan Pablo Duarte? What characteristics would a person need to possess to accomplish the things he did during his lifetime?
- Rice is one of the chief exports of the Dominican Republic. How is it grown? What type of climate is necessary to grow rice? What other areas of the world are known for growing rice? What similarities do these countries have with the Dominican Republic?
- Who is the leader of the Dominican Republic? Is he or she elected, appointed, or brought into office some other way? What rules determine how long this person is in office and what his or her duties are?

Chronology

pre-1492	A succession of Indian tribes lives on the land that is now the Dominican Republic; the Arawak Indians are living there when Europeans first arrive.
1492	Columbus's expedition arrives in the West Indies, and one of the ships, the *Santa María*, runs aground off the northern coast of the island of Hispaniola, near the present-day city of Cap-Haïtien, Haiti.
1496	The settlement of La Nueva Isabela—the present-day Santo Domingo—is established.
early 1500s	Spanish settlers flock to Hispaniola and enslave the Indians; after the Indian population has been decimated by disease and overwork, African slaves are brought to the island.
1511	Antonio de Montesinos, a Dominican friar, preaches against the system of forced Indian labor prevalent on Hispaniola.
1527	Bartolomé de Las Casas, later proclaimed Protector of the Indians by Queen Isabella, enters the Dominican Order.
1697	The Treaty of Ryswick gives France control of the land that is now Haiti; Spain retains control of the land that is now the Dominican Republic.
1795	Spain cedes the colony of Santo Domingo (the present-day Dominican Republic) to France.
1801	Toussaint-Louverture, leader of a successful slave revolt in Haiti, gains control of the entire island of Hispaniola.
1809	Spain regains control of Santo Domingo.
1821	Spain grants independence to Santo Domingo.
1822	Haiti regains control of the entire island of Hispaniola.
1844	Juan Pablo Duarte leads a revolt against Haiti, and the Dominican Republic is officially formed on February 27.
1861	At the request of the Dominican government, Spain begins to govern the country.
1865	Spain leaves the Dominican Republic.
1882–89	Ulises Heureaux rules the country as a dictator, leaving it with huge debts to foreign nations.

1905	The United States takes over collection of customs duties to help oversee repayment of the Dominican Republic's debts.
1916–24	U.S. Marines keep order in the country, maintaining peace between rival political groups.
1930	Rafael Leónidas Trujillo Molina stages a revolution and takes control of the country, ruling as a dictator for the next 30 years.
1961	Trujillo is assassinated, and a power struggle ensues, ending when Juan Bosch is elected president in 1962.
1965	U.S. president Lyndon Johnson sends troops that block the return of Juan Bosch, overthrown in a military coup in 1963.
1966	Joaquín Balaguer is elected president in June, and the last foreign troops leave the country in September; Balaguer will serve for 12 prosperous years, as high sugar prices bring better economic times.
1978	President Balaguer is defeated by Silvestre Antonio Guzmán Fernández.
1986	Balaguer regains the presidency, serving until 1996.
1988	Hurricane Georges strikes the country, killing 200 and forcing thousands from their homes; the storm causes about $1.2 billion in damage.
2000	Rafael Hipólito Mejía Domínguez is elected president.
2001	Researchers discover the smallest known reptile species in the world, the Jaragua lizard, in the Dominican Republic's Jaragua National Park; it would fit on a penny.
2004	With the country suffering through an economic crisis, Leonel Fernández is reelected as president (he had previously held the office from 1996 to 2000).
2007	The Dominican Republic ratifies a free-trade agreement with the United States and five Central American countries on March 1.
2008	In August, Leonel Fernández is sworn in for a second consecutive term as president.

Further Reading/Internet Resources

Chidester, David. *Christianity: A Global History.* San Francisco: Harper, 2000.

Clammer, Paul, and Jens Porup. *Dominican Republic and Haiti.* Lonely Planet, 2008.

Harvey, Sean. *The Rough Guide to the Dominican Republic.* New York: Rough Guides, 2008

Foley, Erin. *Cultures of the World: The Dominican Republic.* New York: Marshall Cavendish, 1995.

Rogers, Lura, and Barbara Radcliffe. *The Dominican Republic.* New York: Children's Press, 1999.

Travel Information

http://www.hispaniola.com
http://www.dr1.com
http://travel.state.gov/travel/cis_pa_tw/cis/cis_1103.html

History and Geography

http://www.countryreports.org/dominicanrepublic.htm
http://memory.loc.gov/frd/cs/dotoc.html
http://www.photius.com/wfb/wfb1999/dominican_republic/dominican_republic_geography.html

Economic and Political Information

https://www.cia.gov/library/publications/the-world-factbook/geos/dr.html
http://www.gksoft.com/govt/en/do.html

Culture and Festivals

http://www.godominicanrepublic.com
http://www.gowealthy.com/article/306/index.asp

Embassy of the Dominican Republic
1715 22nd St., NW
Washington, DC 20008
Tel: 202-332-6280
Fax: 202-265-8057
Web site: http://www.domrep.org
E-mail: embassy@us.serex.gov.do

Dominican Consulate in New York
1501 Broadway, Suite 410
New York, NY 10036
Tel: 212-768-2480
Web site: http://portal.consuladord-ny.org
E-mail: cdny@consuladord-ny.org

Dominican Republic Ministry of Tourism
136 E. 57 St., Suite 803
New York, NY 10022
Tel: 212-588-1012
Toll Free: 1-888-374-6361
Fax: 212-588-1015
Web site: http://www.godominicanrepublic.com
E-mail: drtourismboardny@verizon.net

Index

Index/Picture Credits

Contributors

Senior Consulting Editor **James D. Henderson** is professor of
international studies at Coastal Carolina University. He is the
author of *Conservative Thought in Twentieth Century Latin America:
The Ideals of Laureano Gómez* (1988; Spanish edition *Las ideas de
Laureano Gómez* published in 1985); *When Colombia Bled: A History
of the Violence in Tolima* (1985; Spanish edition *Cuando Colombia se
desangró, una historia de la Violencia en metrópoli y provincia*, 1984);
and coauthor of *A Reference Guide to Latin American History* (2000)
and *Ten Notable Women of Latin America* (1978).

Mr. Henderson earned a bachelor's degree in history from Centenary College of
Louisiana, and a master's degree in history from the University of Arizona. He then
spent three years in the Peace Corps, serving in Colombia, before earning his doctorate
in Latin American history in 1972 at Texas Christian University.

Bob Temple is the president of Red Line Editorial, Inc., an editorial services firm based
in the Minneapolis–St. Paul area. Bob is an award-winning journalist who has enjoyed
a 16-year career in newspapers and online journalism. He is the author of more than 20
nonfiction books for children and young adults, and seven Internet-related titles.